El fogón de RD

Elizabeth Guzman

This publication contains the opinions and ideas of its author. It is intended to provide helpful and informative material on the subjects addressed in the publication. The author and publisher specifically disclaim all responsibility for any liability, loss, or risk, personal or otherwise, which is incurred as a consequence, directly or indirectly, of the use and application of any of the contents of this book.

WRITERS REPUBLIC L.L.C.
515 Summit Ave. Unit R1
Union City, NJ 07087, USA

Website: *www.writersrepublic.com*
Hotline: *1-877-656-6838*
Email: *info@writersrepublic.com*

Ordering Information:
Quantity sales. Special discounts are available on quantity purchases by corporations, associations, and others. For details, contact the publisher at the address above.

Library of Congress Control Number:		2021931927	
ISBN-13:	978-1-63728-067-6	[Paperback Edition]	
	978-1-63728-359-2	[Hardback Edition]	
	978-1-63728-063-8	[Digital Edition]	

Rev. date: 03/09/2021

At the age of 21, I was welcomed to new home for a family who didn't knew me but opened their door to me to give me the opportunity to work with them and provide help and care to their children, through the time and year I when to a lot different stages in my life together with them and at some point it got me here, as I was taking care of one boy the inspiration was born and today I'm giving birth to that wish of this boy on calling me chef Elizabeth, each day without knowing it he push me to write my own recipes book in honor to his wishes I am thankful, thank you Sammy D.

SIDE DISH

Roast Veggies

1 head of broccoli
2 carrots sliced into ovals
2 red onions
1 zucchini green or yellow
2 bell peppers (different colors each)

Dressing

1/3 cup olive oil
1/3 cup soy sauce
2 garlic cloves (minced)
2 tablespoons honey
1 tablespoon Italian seasoning

Directions

- Cube onions and peppers into 1 inch cubes, divide broccoli florets into one inch each one, chop carrots into ovals or so not too thick, do the same with the zucchini.
- Place baking sheet with baking wax paper and cooking spray add all of the vegetables, pour the dressing on top and bake at 400° for 30-35 minutes mixing every 15 minutes.

Note:

- You can add these veggies to couscous or quinoa even a fresh salad it goes very well!

Roasted Carrots Sweet and Sour

9 baby organic carrot cut in half
2 white parsnips carrot cut in half
6 or so to be long strip cut

Dressing

Maple syrup,	4 spoons
1 lemon juice,	3 spoons
olive oil,	3 spoons
salt to taste	

Directions

- Place the carrots on a baking sheet with parchment paper and spray cooking spray on top. Bake 16 minutes on 400 degrees , bring out and pour the dressing on and bake for another 7 minutes you will go crazy over these carrots!

Spinach Rolls

1 box of baby spinach
2 big fat carrots
1 garlic clove, (minced)
1 tablespoon olive oil
½ teaspoon salt
½ teaspoon honey

Direction

- Peel carrot with a peeler, with same peeler make long thick or wide carrot strip.
- Heat a pan with olive oil, garlic and salt and bring spinach to sauté 3 minutes. Take them out of flame in same pot bring carrot strip to get soft on a low flame and add honey to the carrots.
- Wait till carrots and spinach get warm and wear gloves to work with them.
- Make balls with the spinach and carrots. Take a toothpick and press in the center to hold carrots with spinach together. Serve this with anything.

Grilled Zucchini

Ingredients

4 long zucchini's
1 tablespoon oregano
1 garlic clove
2 tablespoon soy sauce
1 tablespoon of honey
2 tablespoon of olive oil

Directions

- Cut the zucchini into long ovals and place them on a baking pan 9 x 13 – in a separate bowl combine, oregano, garlic, soy sauce, honey and olive oil. Mix them very well till everything is well combined. Add it on the zucchini making sure that every piece has sauce on it.
- Place a grilling pan on stove on a medium flame. Add baking spray on the pan and let the zucchini grill for 3 to 4 minutes on each side or at least till you see the mark of the grilling pan on the zucchini , when its done you can enjoy this as a side dish with meat or you can add it to a salad. Enjoy!

Eggplant Boat

2 eggplants cut in half
1 bag of cheddar cheese or cheese of your choice
1 tablespoon black pepper
1 tablespoon of salt
1 tablespoon garlic powder
1 tablespoon of olive oil
1 white onion small cubes
1 jar marinara sauce chunky

Preparation

- Take the eggplant cut them into cubes inside without cutting the skin off, get out all the inside out in a small bowl and add salt, leave it for 30 minutes till water of eggplant is out or sweated. Use a towel to dry eggplant. In a pan add olive oil and white onion to sauté. Add the eggplant cubes and leave it for a few minutes to sauté. Add garlic powder, black pepper and some salt to taste and cook 8 minutes.

- Take this to a separate bowl add the marinara sauce mix it well and pour back into empty eggplant skin. Preheat oven to 400 degrees. Bake on a cookie pan or cookie sheet over parchment paper for 15 minutes add cheese and bake or broil 2 minutes. Enjoy it.

Avocado Pasta

1 avocado
1 box of fettuccine
1 cup of cherry tomatoes
2 garlic cloves minced
½ tablespoon salt
½ teaspoon black pepper

Direction

- Broil the pasta following instructions
  on the box. Smash the avocado, combine with garlic and salt, and add black pepper and stir
  the pasta, pour in the tomatoes and toss it around till all the pasta is green and creamy, serve
  and enjoy it warm.
- This is a perfect side dish for anything.

Arroz con Coco

2 cups of rice

1 teaspoon salt

4 cups coconut milk if milk is too thick use only 2 cups of coconut milk and 2 cups of water, taste the salt and add more if needed.

Direction

- Wash the rice with water, put your rice pot on the stove. Add milk and salt, leave it to boil, when milk is boiling add the rice, same as regular rice, when liquid is absorbed but not completely dry, lower the flame cover pot and let simmer 20 minutes, it's amazing with scrambled eggs.

Cauliflower and Broccoli Casserole

3 garlic cloves, minced
1 head of cauliflower
1 head of broccoli
2 tablespoons of consommé powder
1 small can of evaporated milk
1 pound of shredded cheese of your choice
1 tablespoon salt
1 tablespoon black pepper
3 tablespoon butter
1 white onion
1 tablespoon olive oil

Preparation

- Place broccoli and cauliflower in a bowl and cut into small florets. Place them on a baking pan add olive oil and butter, garlic and salt and bake 6 minutes at 450 degrees mixing every 2 minutes.
- Add consommé powder and evaporated milk (just enough milk to cover the vegetables).
- Preheat oven to 375-400. Sprinkle black pepper cover and bake very tightly for 20 minutes or until milk is absorbed completely. Put cheese on top and now bake uncovered for 6 minutes or until cheese is crispy on top. Serve and enjoy it.

Parsley Potatoes

2 pounds red potatoes (cubed)
1 inch chunk ?
1 tablespoon salt divided
3 garlic clove minced
4 tablespoon olive oil
3 tablespoon parsley flakes or fresh parsley

Preparation

- Take potatoes and wash them with the skin on, cube them into 1 inch size and add water on a pot add salt and take it to cook till its cooked but not too soft, let them cool off.
- In a frying pan, add olive oil and garlic immediately add potatoes to avoid burning garlic (low flame recommended); add parsley flake and mix well, add remaining salt and toss it around serve and enjoy.

Potato Balls (Baked or Fried)

2 pounds Yukon potatoes
1 tablespoon salt
1 tablespoon black pepper
2 ½ tablespoon flour
2 eggs
1 tablespoon paprika
2 ½ tablespoons olive oil

Directions

- Add water to a pot and peel potatoes into chunks and cook till they're soft, pour water out and smash them, add olive oil, paprika, eggs, flavor and salt to taste, take gloves and roll potatoes into balls.
- Take baking pan, spray cooking oil and place each ball on it, preheat oven 425 degrees and take the balls to bake for 20 minutes or until balls are golden orange. Let them cool off and serve with any sauce.
- My sauce is sweet chilly with mayo and some sriracha sauce to make it a little spicy, scallions or cilantro can be used to decorate. Enjoy it.

Alfredo Pasta

½ cup cream milk

3 garlic cloves, minced

½ teaspoon salt

½ teaspoon parsley flakes

¼ cup butter

½ teaspoon black pepper

1 box of pasta of your choice

Directions

- Cook pasta following instructions on box, when pasta is done cooking rinse with cold water
- On a big pan heat on low flame, butter and salt, add the cream milk and black pepper stir and add garlic, raise flame and wait till it starts to boil, lower flame and bring pasta to combine toss around and add parsley flake, perfect with fish or bread. Enjoy it.

Baked Potatoes and Sweet Potatoes

2 Sweet potatoes
4 Idaho potatoes
salt to taste
oil to taste
paprika to taste
black pepper to taste

Directions

- Peel potatoes and sweet potatoes, cut them into 1 inch cubes, place them in a bowl add olive oil, salt, paprika and black pepper, combine very well.
- Take a cookie sheet and spread the potatoes and sweet potatoes very well, pre-heat oven to 375 degrees and when its ready bake them for 35-40 minutes, enjoy it.

MY ROOTS

Chivo Guisado con Chen Chen

5 pounds goat meat on chunks
2 cups of fresh cilantro
10 garlic cloves (minced)
1 green bell pepper sliced long
1 red pepper sliced long
2 red onions sliced round
1 cup sliced olives or whole olives
2 cups of coffee
1 cup rum or whiskey any kind
½ cup oregano ground
½ cup soy sauce
¼ cup tomato paste
1 cup of lime juice
½ cup olive oil, 3 tablespoon adobo goya

Directions for the goat.

- In a big bowl cover the goat with coffee and leave it alone for 30 minutes, afterwards rinse with water, add lime juice and goat should start getting sticky and fatty. Next, take a meat scissor and cut the fatty sticky white slimy fabric on the meat and throw out, rinse with water and add a whiskey teaspoon add 3 tablespoons of adobo goya teas eroun, add olives, 1 red onion, half of the red pepper, half of the green pepper, add oregano and cilantro and soy sauce, leave it alone for 2 hours.

- Now bring a big wide pot to medium high flame with oil, add the meat to sewted without cover stir it around with wooden spoon, goat shout start bringing out its own water when the pot is completely out of liquid end drizzling like frying move around and add 3 cups of water. Leave it alone to cook the water and dry out again.

- Add now 4 to 5 cups of water and leave it to dry out again. Continue this process without a cover about 1 hour to avoid retaining the smell of the goat in the meat itself if you feel it need 2 hours or so do it better.

- Now cover the pot and cook with water on very high flame 2 more hours checking the water and adding more if it needs it, make sure to not burn the meat, test the meat to see if ts soft and has a good salt level, now that your meat is soft and juicy, dry out the water add garlic cloves and the rest of cilantro, onion and peppers sautéed a little to add the flavors of this amazing vegetable add the tomato paste and a little bit of water to not have a dry ending and instead to have juice on your meat now let's cook the chen chen.

Chen Chen

3 cups of peeled, crocked corn
3 tablespoons of butter
5 cups of water
1 tablespoon Consomme powder
½ tablespoon salt

- Rinse corn with abundant water to get rid of stray peels and excess starch.
- Soak the corn in water for 2 hours. Drain corn after.
- Heat the butter on low heat, add corn, and stir until it changes to a dark yellow color.
- Add water with salt and consommé powder and cook on a medium heat till the water is all evaporated. Remove from heat and cover, wait 5 minutes or so, take a fork and fluff around, serve with your goat and you will be crazy about this amazing plate!
- You can also serve it with white rice.

Sancocho Dominicano

2 pounds smoke pork chops or smoke turkey on cube 2 inch size

1 chicken cut on sizes

3 pounds of beef with bones

1 cup of silantro fresh

1 white onion or red big chunk

6 leaves of wide coriander

1 green bell pepper on 4

1 pound of kabocha squash

3 green plantains

4 sopita maggi or consomme powders if you don't have sopita

1 teaspoon oregano for reach meat

2 yokes

2 white Yautie

3 corns on circles 4 inch thick

3 tablespoons of ground ginger.

1 tablespoon salt

3 tablespoons olive oil

10 garlic cloves

1 red onion whole

17

Directions

- In a big soup pot, add oil, heat on low and sauté chicken and beef with oregano, onion, silantro pepper for about 15 minutes, add garlic cloves and sopita maggi continue to saute, add water about 4 cups and cover to cook 30 minutes or so.

- Now on a different pan, sauté smoked pork chops with oregano and salt, drop of oil and simmer on low flame till the flavor is out and smelling delicious, add drop of water, continue to cook few more minutes, now add the smoke chops to the rest of the meat and saute altogether, meantime peel all vegetables cut on 2 inch size, rinse and add to the meat continue to sauteed, add water till oil meat and vegetable are cover, when the kabocha is soft bring out 2 cups of them blend some and add back to the Sancocho, add the coriander leaves and a red onion, taste the salt and add some more if is need it, sprinkle black pepper is optional, add the ground ginder and continue to cook, your meats and vegetable should be soft and good now, taste and serve on a big deep bowl, cook white rice to accompany this dish and add some avocado slices on side, this is heaven on earth I promise you that you will never taste something better.

Arroz con Dulce

Sweet Rice Pudding

2 cups rice jasmine or short grain

1 ½ can coconut milk

1 can evaporated milk

4 sticks of cinnamon

12 whole cloves

1 teaspoon salt

½ cup of sugar

1 cup of raisins

3 cups whole milk

Directions

In a large pot combine whole milk, evaporated milk, and coconut milk, cinnamon sticks, cloves, salt and rice, bring it to boil on a very low flame, while its simmering add sugar and continue to mix keep mixing till the rice seems to absorb all the milk add raisins and add more milk if it needs it continue to stir, when its creamy and rice has cooked and has a soft taste if the rice tastes like coconut milk and smooth is then just serve it on your favorite dish and stick cinnamon sticks in it to decorate or simply use ground cinnamon.

Pastelón de Plátano Maduro

8 yellow plantains not too soft

1 small can of carnation milk or whole milk

1/1 cup margarine butter

2 tablespoon consommé powder

2 tablespoons salt

2 pounds ground beef 10% fat

3 tablespoons paprika powder

3 garlic cloves minced

1 red onion

2 tablespoons tomato paste

3 tablespoons red cooking wine

½ cup green olives

2 cups of cheddar cheese

1 ½ tablespoon olive oil

Directions

- Peel and add to the cooked plantains to water with the consommé powder and 1 tablespoon of salt till the plantains are cooked.
- In a frying pan big enough add olive oil, onion and garlic sauté 3 minutes on a low flames.
- Add met?, paprika, cooking red wine and continue to cook 16 more minutes, add water if the mead need it, add tomato paste, red pepper , green olives and cilantro, taste the salt and add more if you need it. Cook till the meat gets soft and make sure not to leave it watery or with too much liquid inside.
- In the same pot where you cooked the plantain, smash them without water, add butter, milk and salt to taste.
- Take a 9x13 baking dish and make one layer of smashed plantain not too thick not too thin about 1 inch pour in the ground beef and cover with more smashed plantain. Add cheese on top and take it to bake at 375 degrees for about 35 minutes or till starting to smell delicious in your house and gets you hungry. Serve in parties or however you like it.

Kabocha Cream

2 pounds of Kabocha peeled and cut in chunks
1 coconut milk
1 cup of carnation milk
1 ½ cup of sugar
3 ounces of whiskey
2 tablespoons of ground cinnamon
Whipping cream and caramel on jars

Directions

- Take Kabocha to boiling water and cook till it softens. Remove from water. In a blender add some Kabocha some carnation milk and some coconut milk, blend all together make sure its not liquate add some cinnamon powder and sugar.
- Take a glass cup pour some add some whiskey to the bottom
- Cover with whipping cream and caramel, sprinkle ground cinnamon and serve on your favorite holiday.

Habichuelas con Dulce

1 Bag of red beans
1 ½ cup of sugar
1 box of crausings (small)
1 pound of Japanese jam
6 sticks of cinnamon
1 can of carnation milk
1 can of coconut milk
1 gallon of whole milk
1 tablespoon of butter
1 pinch of salt

Directions

- Take the beans with 3 cinnamon sticks to cook with water till beans get softs.
- On a separate pot, peel and cut the Japanese jam on 1inch cube and take it to cook on water with 1 cinnamon stick till the Japanese jam is soft but not too soft.
- Take soft bean to blender with milk and blender till is good to use a strainer to pour inside a big pot, continue to blend all your beans till everything is thing and well combined, add 3 remaining stick of cinnamon and turn on the flame on low, add sugar and stir gradually to make sure that is not burning on bottom, when is hot add in coconut milk and carnation milk, add Japanese jam and crousing take a small cup and taste the sugar make sure is sweet enough if need some more add 1 more cup and a pinch of salt, add the butter and leave it, continue to stir, taste one more time if is good sever and pour some mari cookies on top if you can find them animal cracker works the same, enjoy it.
- Suggestion (add cinnamon powder if it need some more)

Flan of eggs

6 big eggs
1 condense milk
1 cup carnation milk
½ cup of sugar
½ cup of water
½ tablespoon vanilla extract

Directions

- Take to a low flame ½ cup water with sugar don't mx or move leave it alone to make a caramel, when its light brown close the flame pour in a baking and cool it completely. Set aside.
- On a blender add eggs, carnation milk and condense milk, pour vanilla extract, blend very well but not too much to avoid bubbles, poor mixture on coated baking pan with caramel
- Pour water around it or what its called Maria bath
- Preheat oven at 350 degrees when it reaches the right temperate cover it tightly and bake for 1 hour.
- Bring out of oven, uncover and remove from water leave it alone to cool off, when its cold take it to the fridge overnight serve next day on your favorite plate, flip and enjoy it.

Yogurt Cup

18 ounces of vanilla yogurt

10 strawberries cut up

½ cup honey

½ pecans glazed or regular

3 tablespoons of oat

Directions

- Place cupcake holder on cupcake pan. Add in yogurt mixture with honey, pecans, strawberries and oat. Take it to the freezer overnight. Comeback take it out and serve like a refreshing treat.

Dulce de Coco

3 cups of young coconut cut into strips
1 can evaporated milk
2 cups whole milk
1 can condensed milk
1 pinch of salt
1 teaspoon vanilla extract
1-2 cinnamon sticks

Directions

- Take to low flame evaporated milk, whole milk, condensed milk, add salt, vanilla and cinnamon stick, place the coconut in the pot of milk and let it cook on very low for 20-30 minutes stirring occasionally to avoid burning the bottom, when the mixture starts to get stuck and heavy use a wooden spoon and move every 2 minutes, close the flame and leave it to cool off then serve cold and enjoy it!

Majarete

2 cups whole milk
3 sticks cinnamon
½ ground nutmeg
2 cans of corn goya
1 can coconut milk
1 cup of sugar
¼ cup cornstarch

Directions

- In a medium pot pour in the whole milk, cinnamon stick and nutmeg to simmer cover it on a low flame for 10 minutes.
- On a blender, blend the corn without water, coconut milk, sugar and cornstarch till it gets smooth using a strainer, strain mixture to the previous pot with whole milk making sure there aren't not pieces inside.
- Turn the flame back on to low, with a wooden spoon, mix the mixture and continue to move and stir till it is starts to get heavy about to boil and bubbly close the flame and add portion to cup or serving bowls, leave it to cool off, when it's cold, take it to the fridge for 8 hours, serve and enjoy it.
- Note (not necessary you can enjoy it while its warm too)
- My favorite way is warm I got to taste of flavors.

Mangú con 3 Golpes

3 green plantains
½ cup butter
2 eggs
½ oil
8 slices of salami
4 slices of frying cheese
1 red onion on circles
½ teaspoon salt
½ teaspoon lime juice
1 table spoon white vinegar
¾ butter
salt ½ tablespoon

Directions

- Peel plantain, take a pot with water and salt and bring your plantain to cook for 25-30 minutes add more water after 20 minutes cooking , close flame completely.
- Heat oil and fry the salami and right after fry the eggs, make sure your salami is golden or brownish on the edges.
- Now add vinegar, salt and lime juice to your onion, leave it there 5 minutes.
- Heat a pan with ¾ butter and add onions to cook with the butter and fry.
- Remove the water from the plantains, add ½ spoon of butter and smash very well, serve on a plate with salami and egg, meanwhile, fry the cheese in slices also, when its done add it to the plate, place onions on the top of the mangú and decorate with some delicious avocado.

Chambre Dominicano

3 tablespoons canola oil

2 minced garlic cloves

1 teaspoon dry oregano

1 small red onion diced

1 can red pinto beans

1 cup long ground rice uncooked

2 bay leaves

4 cilantro leaves or coriander leaves

1 ½ cup kabocha squash 1inch cubes peeled

1 pound smoke pork chops excess of fat removed and cut on chunks

4 cups of water

1 tablespoon consommé powder

juice of one sour orange

salt and pepper to taste

1 green plantain cut into small circles

Directions

- Place oil in a rice pot.
- Add consommé powder, garlic, onion, salt and oregano, turn flame on to medium and bring smoke chops to sauté with them.
- Lower the flame, cover pot and cook 35 minutes with a drop of water, add the remaining ingredient to sewded and bring the 4 cups of water cut till the rice is soft but has not absorbed all the liquid once its done serve with avocado you won't need anything else.

Pescado con Coco

½ cup tomato paste
2 red snapper fish
1 can coconut milk
1 table spoon consommé powder
¼ cup cilantro
4 minced garlic cloves
1 red onion
½ green pepper
½ tablespoon oregano
1 tablespoon olive oil

Directions

- Take your fish and cover with oregano.
- Take a pot to a low flame add olive oil, garlic, consommé powder, cilantro, pepper and onion and sauté, add tomato paste and sauté a total of 3 minutes to 5, add coconut milk and a little bit of water, bring fish to cook inside the milk and add the flavor to it. Serve with white rice.

Moro de Guandules

2 cups of rice
4 cups of water
½ teaspoon salt
2 garlic cloves minced
¼ cup olive sliced
½ green bell pepper
1 small purple onion sliced
1 teaspoon consommé powder
¼ cilantro chopped small
1 tablespoon olive oil
2 cans of green peas
1 tablespoon tomato paste

Directions

- In a rice pot add in the oil, onion, garlic, olives, consommé powder and salt, turn the flame onto medium and sauté 3 – 5 minutes, add green peas, tomato paste and pepper continue to saute 3 more minutes, add cilantro and 4 cups of water.
- On a different bowl rinse rice with water.
- When peas are boiling add the rice without the water and stir.
- When rice seems to be absorbing almost all the water, cover the pot and simmer the rice for about 20 minutes when its done serve your rice with your favorite fish or meat.

Pastelon de Papa Y Queso

15 yuka potatoes sliced on circles
2 pounds of cheddar cheese or mozzarella cheese shredded
1 can of cream milk or evaporated milk
2-3 tablespoon consommé powder
1 tablespoon salt
¼ cup fresh parsley chopped

Directions

- Wash potatoes and slice into circles and take it to boil on water till potatoes are soft and cooked.
- Rinse with water and leave it to cool off.
- Take evaporated milk and add consommé powder 2 tablespoons (of it).
- Place on the flame to warm up
- When its dissolved, take it off the flame.
- Take a baking dish and put on a layer of sliced potatoes, Pour some milk consume mixture on top making sure it's covered and add cheese on top about 1 ½ inch thick add more potatoes and more cheese some more milk and bake at 400 degrees for 35 minutes, cover it very tightly. Finally take it out and broil the cheese 2 more minutes, use the parsley for decoration on top. Enjoy it.

Coconut Flan

2 cups of coconut milk
½ cup carnation milk
1 tablespoon ground cinnamon
1 teaspoon vanilla extract
2 eggs
4 tablespoons of cornstarch
1 cup of sugar

Directions

- In a pot on low flame add coconut milk, cinnamon, carnation milk, sugar and stir slow.
- In a separate bowl add eggs and blend on a blender with cornstarch add to the pot and continue to mix till it starts to boil, close the flame.
- Make a caramel with one cup of sugar and ½ cup of water, don't touch or mix till its brown on a high flame, pour in a pan let it cool off, add coconut mixture and leave it in fridge overnight.
- Serve the following day and sprinkle sliced almonds to decorate your flan.

Arepa de mi Abuela Torta

Ingredients

3 bananas

3 cups of sugar

1 pinch of salt

1 teaspoon lime zest

4 cups whole milk

¼ cup butter

½ raisins

1 can coconut milk

1 can carnation milk

Caramel 2 pounds or 32 ounce

1 teaspoon baking soda

4 big eggs

1 teaspoon vanilla extract

Directions

- On a blender combine bananas and 2 cups of milk, blend till everything is very smooth, in a big bowl add your banana and milk mix, bring the rest of the remaining ingredients and stir very well, move to combine everything evenly.
- Preheat oven at 350 degrees, once its reached the right temperature, pour the mixture on the baking sheet, and take it to bake for 45 minutes until it gets golden brown on top. Taste and enjoy it.

Kabocha Squash Flan

16 ounces kabocha squash, peeled and cut on cubes

3 eggs

2 large yolks?

7 tablespoons of white sugar

¾ milk

¾ heavy cream

1 ½ teaspoons vanilla extract

8 cups boiling water

Directions

- Preheat oven at 350 degrees meanwhile, make the caramel. In a small pan combine ¾ cup sugar with 3 tablespoon of water boil it till the sugar starts to turn light brown, don't mix or stir leave it to cook alone, remove from pan and add to the 9x13 or round dish where you're making the flan move to coat the entire bottom. Set aside.
- Add the kabocha squash to a medium heat on a pot till it gets soft, in a different bowl, add eggs, egg yolks and heavy cream whisk till its well combined, add vanilla extract and sugar and stir to combine, transfer eggs combination to a blender and add some kabocha squash to blend all together till its all smooth. Pour in the dish where you're making the caramel, add the pan over another pan halfway in water make sure water is warm cover tightly then add to the oven to bake for 35 minutes or 40 minutes or till you see bubbles on top the bring it out let it cool off and leave it in the fridge overnight. Place them on a plate and serve. Enjoy it.

Oatmeal Breakfast

2 sticks of cinnamon

1 tablespoon of cloves

1 ½ cup of oatmeal old fashion

2 cups for milk

1 cup carnation milk

½ teaspoon butter

1 cup of sugar

Directions

- Bring a pot to a medium flame with carnation milk, milk, cinnamon, cloves and sugar and add butter. Stir and add oatmeal to boil all together, when the oatmeal boils and the milk seems to look creamy close the flame and enjoy it.
- Oatmeal texture should be really soft.

SOUP

Zucchini Soup

2 tablespoons olive oil

6 zucchini's

8 ounces broccoli fresh or frozen

8 ounces cauliflowers

1 ½ tablespoon consommé powder

1 big diced onion

3 sticks diced celery

4 mince garlic cloves

½ tablespoon black pepper

½ tablespoon salt

water

Directions

- Bring olive oil to a big soup pot, add onions and open flame to medium level to sauté with celery for 8 minutes, add broccoli and cauliflower.
- Cut zucchini into big chunks add to the rest of ingredients together with consommé powder salt and black pepper. Sauté others 5 minutes and add water till vegetables are covered or just enough to be swimming in the saute. Cook on low flame 45 minutes.
- With a stick blender, blend your soup. Serve and enjoy this with anything.

Roasted Butternut Squash Soup

1 butternut squash (big and long)

1 sweet potato

3 carrots

2 big onions

1 tablespoon salt

2-3 sticks celery

1 tablespoon consommé powder

1 tablespoon parsley flakes

1 tablespoon olive oil

Direction

- Pre-heat oven to 375 degrees. Cut butternut squash in half, place it on a baking sheet over parchment paper and bake for 35 minutes on one side then 15 minutes on other size.
- Add oil and onion to sauté on a deep soup pot with a low flame, cut celery into medium chunks and add it in, peel carrot and add, peel sweet potato and cut into chunks.
- Add in, take kabocha out of oven, remove seeds, with a spoon take the inside of the Kabocha and add to the pot, bring water and add till it covers the inside of the pot, add consommé powder, salt and black pepper, cover and cook for 30 minutes.
- Close the flame let it cool off take a hand blender and when its cool blend it. Taste the salt add more if its needed. Turn on heat and warm up to serve. Sprinkle parsley flake on each portion.

Cauliflower Soup

1 bag of frozen cauliflower
2 Idaho potatoes cut into 1 inch cubes
1 carrot chunk
3 sticks of celery
1 whole head of garlic
2 tablespoons of consommé powder
1 big onion
salt and black pepper to taste
2 tablespoons olive oil

Directions

- Heat the oil on a soup pot. Add onion and celery, saute for 5 – 8 minutes add the carrot and cauliflower, pour in the potatoes and add water till everything is covered in water, cover and cook for 15 minutes. Add consommé powder black pepper and salt and continue to cook for 15 more minutes.
- Preheat oven to 400 degrees. Cover with foil and roast for 30 minutes.
- Close the flame on the soup and leave it to cool off a little bit, take a hand blender and check if you need to remove water before blending. Blend the soup and taste the salt add more if need it Take out garlic and squeeze out the juice of the garlic into the soup taste and serve with your favorite croutons.

Vegetable Soup

1 cup of Kabocha squash

2 zucchini's

3 carrots

1 white parsnip carrot

1 cup of oatmeal

3 stick scelery

1 big onion

2 tablespoons consommé powder

½ tablespoon salt

black pepper to taste

½ tablespoon of paprika

2 tablespoons olive oil

Directions

- Peel Carrots and cut into small cubes, wash zucchini with skin and cut it into cubes, add diced celery and onions. Peel Kabocha squash and cube it small too.
- In a big soup pot add the oil to heat with onion, sauté all the vegetable for 10 minutes add in spices and water till vegetables are covered in water.
- Leave it to cook for 10 minutes with the cover on and add consommé powder. Taste and add the oatmeal on it. Let it cook 8 more minutes if water is needed. Add some more black pepper and salt and cook 2 more minutes, serve and enjoy it.

SALAD

Potatoe Salad

1 pound yellow potatoes peeled and cubed in a small size
½ cup scallion only green part
½ cup red onion tiny cutes
½ cup fresh cilantro chopped small.
2 egg whites cooked and cubed

Dressing

3 tablespoon mayonnaise
3 tablespoon white sugar
½ tablespoon sea salt

Directions

- Add water and potatoes with 1 tablespoon salt to cook in a pot, when the potatoes are cooked but not too soft remove them from the water and leave it alone to cool off.
- Once potatoes are cold add red onions cilantro, scallions and mix it well, add egg whites and mix some more.
- Prepare dressing and add to the potatoes, taste the salt to make sure it's properly salted, if not add some more salt, serve and enjoy.
- Note:
- If your salad is too dry add olive oil , this is optional, the salad comes out very smooth.

Ribbon Salad

1 box of spring mix
2 carrots sliced in ribbons
1 red onion on half slice
1 cup of white mushroom on slice

Dressing

3 tablespoons maple syrup
3 tablespoons olive oil
3 tablespoons lemon
1 garlic clove
½ tablespoon salt

Preparation

- In a big bowl, combine the spring mix, carrots, onion and white mushroom together, don't mix too much to avoid getting the salad soggy.
- Pour dressing on top and enjoy!

Corn Salad

2 cans of corn
1 cup cherry tomatoes
1/3 cup sliver almonds
½ cup fresh dill

Dressing

3 tablespoons olive oil
3 tablespoons lemon juice
½ cup fresh chopped dill not the pole only leaf
½ tablespoon salt
black pepper to taste
½ ground ginger

Preparation

- In a bowl combine corn, cherry tomatoes, silver almonds and fresh dill, toss around and pour the dressing to combine very well. Serve and enjoy.

44

Carrot, Cabbage and Radish Salad

1 cup of sliced radish
1 cup of red cabbage sliced
1 cup of shredded carrot
1 red onion chopped into circles
1 yellow pepper cut into 1 inch strips

Dressing

2 tablespoon olive oil
2 tablespoon salt
1 pinch black pepper
2 tablespoon lemon

Directions

- In a medium bowl combine radish, red cabbage, shredded carrots, red onions and yellow peppers, mix very well, pour the remaining ingredient inside and toss it around, serve with your favorite fish and enjoy it.

Spinach, Strawberry Salad

1 cup of strawberries cut into 4 pieces
1 avocado
½ cup red cabbage
½ cup sliced almond
½ yellow pepper sliced long
½ cup with mushroom
1 boxy baby spinach

Dressing
¼ cup mayonnaise
¼ cup olive oil
½ lemon
¼ maple syrup
½ tablespoon salt
½ tablespoon black pepper

Directions

- Combine red cabbage, strawberry, yellow paper, almonds, mushroom and baby spinach.
- Set aside a sliced avocado to put on top.

- Prepare the dressing and pour it on top of your salad.
- Place the avocado and serve right away. ***This salad doesn't last long in the fridge***. Enjoy it.

Russia Salad

1 can small cubed beets (fresh beets)
1 pound of cooked potatoes cubed and
chopped small
1 red onion diced small
½ can green peas
½ cup corn

Dressing

½ cup mayonnaise
½ tablespoon salt
½ tablespoon black pepper
1 tablespoon olive oil

Directions

- In 2 separate pots put the cubed potatoes and beets in small cubes, boil them. The beets will need 2-3 hours of cooking while the potatoes only need 25-30 minutes don't let the potatoes get too soft.
- When the potatoes are cold and cooked combine them with the beets. Add onions and green peas, if you're using a can of green peas rinse them well, if your using frozen peas steam them 3 minutes, add the corn and mix very well.
- Pour the dressing on top and stir, serve and enjoy it.

Mango / Arugula Salad

1 box baby arugula
1 red onion ½ sliced thin
½ cup radish sliced in half
1 cup of mango (not soft)
1 cup of raspberry (cleaned)

Dressing

½ cup plain green yogurt
¼ extra virgin olive oil
¼ cup Dijon mustard
4 tablespoon honey
3 tablespoon lemon juice
2 tablespoon apple cider vinegar
1 clove garlic minced
½ tablespoon salt
½ tablespoon ground ginger

Directions

- In a big bowl combine the radish, red onion, mango, raspberries and arugula.
- Don't mix it too much, on a different cup combine the dressing mix it very well and pour on each portion of salad that you serve. Enjoy the primavera salad.

Macaroni Salad

½ cup macaroni
½ cup corn
½ cup red onion diced small
1 can of tuna
½ cup fresh cilantro
1 red pepper diced

Dressing

¼ cup white sugar
¼ cup mayonnaise
2 tablespoons salt
½ tablespoon black pepper

Directions

- Pour the macaroni to cook in water and salt till they're well cooked. Let them cool off.
- In a bowl combine the red onion, corn, tuna and mix very well then add in the macaroni and mix till it's well combined. Add a red pepper and continue mixing.
- Add the mayonnaise, white vinegar, salt and black pepper, mix very well, Finally, add the fresh cilantro, taste the salt and take it to the fridge for 2 hours. When its cold serve and enjoy.

Cucumber Salad

2 egg tomatoes in small cubes
1 long persion on small cubes
1 small white onion diced tiny
½ cup fresh cilantro

Dressing

1 lime
3 tablespoon olive oil
½ tablespoon salt
pinch of black pepper

- Combine cucumber, tomatoes, white onion and cilantro, add lime, olive oil, salt and black pepper.

- Note: This is perfect for tacos red meat or simple and as an extra dish.

(Turkey)

Penne / Pastrami Salad

1 Box Penne

1 bunch of scallion, sliced

½ green bell pepper

2 tablespoons dried parsley flakes

1 cup cherry tomatoes

1 red onion

1 pound of pastrami (Turkey) small cubes

parmesan cheese optional, I didn't use it.

Dressing

Olive oil to taste

Salt to taste

black pepper to taste

Preparation

- Pour water in a pot to boil. Add salt if you like and cook the penne pasta following instructions on the box.
- When pasta is cooked rinse with cold water.
- Place pasta on big bowl add green pepper, onion, cherry tomatoes, sliced scallion (the little of green part) and drop out of the water, make sure the scallions are 3-4 inches long the scallion. Dried Parsley flakes, cube the turkey pastrami and add to your pasta also.
- Dress with olive oil, salt and pepper and serve it while its warm and you will love this interesting pasta salad that won't need an additional dish.

Black Olive Macaroni Salad

1 cup macaroni
1 cup black olives sliced
1 cup red bell pepper (tiny cubes)
1 cup fresh parsley chopped (only leaves)

Dressing

½ cup mayonnaise
½ cup white wine vinegar
½ cup white sugar
½ tablespoon salt
½ tablespoon black pepper
1 tablespoon olive oil

Directions

- Take a big pot add about 6 cups of water, add ½ tablespoon salt and take it to the flame to boil, once its boiling cook the macaroni for 10 minutes or so, follow instructions on the box.
- When macaroni's are cooked remove from flame and rinse with cold water.
- Add red pepper, black sliced olives fresh parsley and toss around.
- In a separate bowl mix the dressing ingredients very well.
- Pour everything on your salad and take it to the fridge for 1 hour or till is cold
- Serve on a very hot day to have empty plates, enjoy it.

Guacamole of my Heart

8 cherry tomatoes

2 hass avocados

1/3 tbsp. salt

½ tsp. black pepper

2 tablespoons lime juice

1 tablespoon chopped cilantro

1 small challed onion diced

Directions

- Smash the avocado, add onion, tomatoes, cilantro, salt, pepper, onion and lime juice mix and server with tacos, crackers or bread etc.

Baby Arugula with Purple Cabbage and Tofu or Chicken

Ingredients

2 tablespoons olive oil

1 box baby arugula

½ red or purple cabbage

1 cup croutons of your choice

6 slices of tofu or chicken cutlets

3 clove garlic

3 tablespoon soy sauce

2 tablespoon honey

Dressing

3 tablespoons mayonnaise

3 tablespoons soy sauce

3 tablespoon olive oil

2 tablespoon honey

1 pinch of black pepper

Directions

- In a big bowl combine the arugula and red cabbage, pour croutons on top to stay fluffy.
- Dress the chicken with honey and soy sauce, add 3 cloves of garlic and 2 tablespoons of olive oil.
- Place a grilling pan on the flame.
- On a medium heat, grill chicken or tofu till its cooked well.
- Let them cool off a little bit and cut them into 1inch cubes.
- Add to the salad, dress and enjoy it.

Simple Romaine Avocado Grilled Chicken Salad

Ingredients

10 chicken cutlets, (thinly sliced)

2 heart of Romaine lettuce

1 ½ avocado

1 tablespoon honey

3 cloves garlic

2 tablespoon soy sauce

1 yellow onion sliced

2 tablespoon olive oil

Dressing

4 tablespoon balsamic vinegar

4 tablespoon olive oil

½ tablespoon salt

¼ tablespoon black pepper

1 tablespoon Dijon mustard

Directions

- Wash and cut romaine lettuce into small cubes or 2inch sized cubes. Cube avocado and add to the lettuce.
- In a separate bowl season the cutlets with garlic, honey, soy sauce, oil and yellow onions.
- Take a grilling pan to a medium flame and spray it with baking spray or cooking spray, when it's hot add chicken cutlets 5 at a time and grill for 4 minutes on each side or till its cooked and marked with grilling pan lines, when its ready, slice each and add to the romaine salad, pour dressing on top and enjoy it.

Chickpea Salad

Ingredients

1 can chickpea
1 Persian cucumber long cut in half circles
1 egg tomatoes (diced)
1 red union (diced)
½ fresh cilantro chopped
½ tablespoon salt
½ tablespoon black pepper
1 lime
2 tablespoon virgin olive oil
1 hass avocado (optional)
1 green or yellow bell pepper, small cubes

Directions (16 minutes)

- Serving – 4 bowls
- Step 1
- In a big bowl, combine all the ingredients, stir to combine very well, add the salt and pepper and oil, mix and add the lime, after everything is ready and prepared to serve you can top with avocado slices or you use feta cheese, chicken, tofu or even steak strips to have extra protein with this amazing delicious easy and fresh salad. Enjoy

Fresh Broccoli Salad

Ingredients

1 head of fresh raw broccoli thinly sliced
½ of a red cabbage sliced thin
1 carrot sliced in a long strip
1 cup of cranberries dried
1 cup of mix nuts of your choices

Dressing

½ cup mayonnaise
½ cup white sugar
½ cup white vinegar

Directions

- In a big bowl – mix broccoli, red cabbage, carrot, dry cranberries and mix nuts very well, pour the dressing on top and place it in the fridge for 2 hours to get well combined. Afterwards serve on your favorite dish and enjoy it.

Simple Tomato Salad

3 eggs tomatoes (cubed)
1 cup red cabbage thinly sliced
3 Persian cucumbers cubed
½ cup chopped cilantro

Dressing

1/3 cup olive oil
2 cloves garlic
3 tablespoons maple syrup
1 whole lime

Directions

- In a bowl combine the red cabbage sliced thinly with egg tomatoes sliced into small cubes, add cucumber and chopped cilantro, mix them well.
- Prepare the dressing in a separate bowl, combine very well and pour over the salad, let it sit in your fridge for 20 minutes and enjoy it.

Kale, Tomato Salad

1 box fresh kale
1 cup cherry tomatoes
1 sweet potato, roasted (with skin)
½ cup sunflower seeds
½ avocado in slices

Dressing

3 tablespoon olive oil
3 tablespoon lime juice
½ tablespoon salt
½ tablespoon black pepper
1 ½ tablespoon honey

Step 1

- Wash and cut the sweet potatoes, spray them with cooking spray, sprinkle flake paprika and garlic and power on them. Roast in the oven at 375° for 35 minutes.
- While it's baking, prepare kale in a bowl, cut cherry tomatoes in half and add to the kale.
- Sprinkle with sunflower seeds and add the sliced avocado. When the sweet potatoes are done, let them cool off and add to your salad.
- Pour the dressing on top and you will love it.

POULTRY

Mushroom Chicken Cutlets

6 small thinly sliced chicken cutlets
1 cup of diced mushrooms
1 small white onion
3 cloves of minced garlic
1 tablespoon of soy sauce
1 tablespoon of olive oil
2 ½ tablespoons of flour

Directions

- Place the cutlets soy sauce, garlic and honey, on a frying pan on low flame pour the olive oil and start to cook the chicken 4 minutes on each side.
- After its cooked place the chicken on a separate pan now bring onions and mushrooms to sauté, add some water and pour in the flour to thicken it when its cooked add some salt and black pepper taste pour this on top of your chicken and enjoy it with some potatoe sheds a salad.

Steak with Veggies Paste

Steak of your choice

salt to taste
garlic powder to taste
onion powder to taste
crushed pepper to taste
paprika to taste
3 carrot on julienne
2 table spoon parsley flakes

Directions

- Take the meat and sprinkle all the spices on top on both sides, prepare grilling pan add olive oil and grill the meat for 7-8 minutes each side on medium light, when its well cooked take it out.
- Take the julienne carrot and grill them on the same grilling pan for 3 minutes while tossing it around add salt and parsleys flakes, serve and enjoy.

Lamb Chops

Your best choice

6 lamb chops
3 minced garlic cloves
3 tablespoons paprika
3 tablespoons onion powder
1 tablespoon BBQ sauce
Fresh parsley for decoration with vegetable butter
3 tablespoons for olive oil
2 big onion yellow

Directions

- On a big frying pan, add olive oil on medium flame. Cover chop with paprika, garlic, onion powder, ground ginger and place them on cooking oil to fry on each size for 8 minutes or so and onion to fry inside and add flavor. Take them out of the frying pan and place them on a baking sheet, brush BBQ sauce on each side, cover both completely.
- Bake for 12-15 minute on 400 degrees over the onions
- Uncover and let them bake 5 more minutes, test it with a knife to make sure is cooked bring it out and pour butter, and parsley to serve, smashed potatoes goes very well same as salad.

Sirloin Squirts

2 tbsp. sesame seeds

2 pounds of sirloin steak

2 ½ tablespoons teriyaki sauce

1 tablespoon salt

1 tablespoon black pepper

1 tablespoon garlic powder

1 red onion on big chunks

¼ cup scallions green part

3 tablespoon olive oil

Directions

- Cut sirloin on 1 inch cube, add salt, black pepper, garlic powder add oil on a big frying pan to heat on medium heat, sauté sirloin cubes for 15 minutes adding water if need it, When meat is cooked inside, leave it alone to cool off. Take the tongs and add one piece on steak add one onion chunk till it is fulfilled, brush each side with teriyaki sauce and place it on a grill or grilling pan if you have one, let it cook 3 minutes each side, bring it out and sprinkle with sesame seeds and scallions serve and enjoy it.
- My recommendation is to eat with corn on the cob.

Asparagus with Skirt Steak

2 heads of Asparagus
2 packages of skirt steak
1 tablespoon of paprika
1 tablespoon of honey
1 tablespoon of olive oil
1 tablespoon garlic power

Directions

- Take the skirt steak and add paprika, honey, olive oil and garlic powder.
- Take one Asparagus and roll it with each piece of meat on your grill or grilling pan, spray cooking spray and grill on medium h till everything is well cooked and juicy.

Skirt Steak Tacos

1 bag of soft corn tortillas
1 red onion
3 tablespoon teriyaki sauce
3 garlic cloves minced
1 jalapeño pepper
½ cup fresh cilantro
1 sliced green lime
2 tablespoons of olive oil

Directions

- Take the meat brush it with teriyaki sauce and garlic and take it to the grill for 10 minutes
- 5 minutes on each side or so.
- On frying pan add oil and onion and sauté till they're juicy.
- Cut the meat and warm up the tortillas, add the meat inside, slice some peppers and add cilantro, onion, and a of sprinkle lime juice, enjoy!

Roasted Chicken with BBQ

1 cup BBQ sauce
6 thick boneless chicken cutlets
1 tablespoon garlic powder
1 tablespoon paprika
½ tablespoon salt
½ cup scallions sliced
3 tablespoon olive oil
1 big red onion on circles

Directions

- In a bowl, place the chicken cutlets then add garlic powder, paprika, salt, scallions and red onion.
- In a big frying pan add olive oil and heat on medium heat, bring cutlets to sauté for 5 minutes each side with onions and scallions.
- Prepare a baking sheet with parchment paper, place the cutlets and add BBQ sauce, cover tight and bake at 375 degrees for 25 minutes, uncover cutlets and broil 3-5 minutes.
- Go with everything.

Chicken with Paprika and Honey

1 whole chicken
1 cup of honey
1 red onion diced
2 garlic cloves minced
½ teaspoon ground ginger
½ teaspoon chili powder
Fresh Thyme
-garlic powder to taste
-paprika to taste
-black pepper to taste
-olive oil to cover chicken
-salt to taste

Directions

- Place chicken on parchment paper over a baking sheet, sprinkle salt, garlic powder, paprika, black pepper and olive oil making sure its completely covered, preheat the oven on 375 degrees and cover chicken very tightly with heavy dirty foil bake 1 ½ hour.
- On a frying pan, add 2 tablespoons of olive oil, garlic and red onion, sauté for 3 minutes, add honey, ginger, chili powder and cook till mixture starts boiling.
- When the chicken finishes cooking, bring it out and spill out all the water brush it with the sauce you made turn oven up to 400 degrees and bake the chicken uncovered for 10 minutes turn on the broil option and broil it for 3 minutes enjoy with it corn and smashed potatoes or rice.
- Thyme is for decoration only.

White Wine Chicken Cutlets

½ tablespoon salt

6 big chicken cutlets boneless

1 cup of white cooking wine or dry wine

½ cup consommé powder

4 cloves of minced garlic.

4 cup of water or 3 depends on pan

½ cup basil leaves for decoration

3 tablespoon flour

2 bay leaves

1 white onion big on circles

½ tablespoon black pepper

1 tablespoon oil

Directions

- Take a big pan add oil, garlic and onion to sauté on low evolving garlic, add the consommé powder and flour, add water and bay leaves, bring cutlets, wine and salt and black pepper, simmer on low flame for 45 minutes this chicken goes very well with vegetables and potatoes.

Meat over Eggplants

1 pound of beef brisket

1 cup of BBQ sauce

1 big onion sliced

½ teaspoon garlic powder

½ teaspoon paprika

½ teaspoon salt

½ teaspoon black pepper

1 yellow pepper long strip

1 small red onion sliced

1 cup marinara sauce

1 big eggplant

Directions

- Place brisket on a baking sheet with parchment pepper, add sliced onion, salt, paprika, garlic powder and black pepper, making sure that it's covering the meat, and add BBQ sauce over your meat.
- Preheat oven at 300 degrees, cover meat very tightly and bake 2 hours or till meat is soft inside and you can work with it.
- Take eggplant and slice in big circles, sprinkle salt and garlic powder, heat on a frying pan with olive oil and fry eggplant 3 minutes each side. Don't overcook!
- Bring ½ cup of marinara sauce to another baking sheet and place fried eggplant on top.
- Divide the meat into long strips brush eggplant on top with the remaining marinara sauce, add meat and sliced yellow pepper with red onions, bake on broil setting for 4 minutes, enjoy this fancy dish.

Stuffed Pepper with Chicken

Ingredients

Cook time: 20 minutes

Preparation: 6 minutes

3 bell pepper of your choices

Serving: 6 cups

1 pound of boneless chicken cutlet

1 small red onion diced

3 garlic cloves

3 tablespoon of soy sauce

10 ounces or broccoli florets

2 tablespoon of olive oil

½ poon of cheddar cheese (optional)

Preparation

- (step 1)
- Cut peppers in half, remove and discord the tops, seeds and membranes of the bell peppers. Arrange peppers in a baking dish. Spray baking oil on top.
- (Step 2)
- Combine broccoli, onion, garlic cloves, arrange the on a frying pan with the olive oil and sauté the broccoli, onion and garlic on a medium flame for 3 minutes.
- (Step 3)
- Cut the chicken on small cubes ½ inch or so, add the soy sauce and combine with previous mix of broccoli and sauté for another 8 minutes till chicken starts to get golden edges.
- (Step 4)
- Add mixture of chicken on pepper already prepared on baking dish, stuff each one very well.
- Preheat oven on 425° once it reaches the right temperature bake the stuffed pepper for 10 minutes add cheese if you'd like and bake 2 more minutes. Enjoy!

Stuffed Sweet Potatoes

Salt and black pepper to taste
4 long sweet potatoes
1 ½ pound ground beef 10% fat
1 egg tomatoe
1 red onion
2 tablespoon tomato paste
2 cloves of minced garlic
½ cup water

Directions

- wash it, and wrapped with skin on foil paper, bake on 375° 2 hours.
- On a big pan, add meat, onion and tomato, leave to cook on low flame 12 minutes, add water ½ cup, tomato paste, salt and pepper to taste, cook till meat is well cooked, add if need gradually.
- Take the sweet potato out, make a long wedge inside without breaking sweet potatoes.

- Pour inside the ground beef and add some green peppers and lettuce if you like this is a complete dinner or lunch enjoy it.

FISH

Spicy Salmon

4 slices of salmon
1 cup mayonnaise
½ cup sriracha sauce
½ table spoon salt
½ teaspoon black pepper
1 lemon juice
black sesame seeds or thyme (optional)

Directions

- Combine the mayonnaise, sriracha sauce, salt and pepper in a cup and mix very well.
- Preheat oven on 357° Take an orange baking sheet with parchment paper and pour in the salmon with the lemon juice.
- With a brush, brush the mayonnaise mixture on each piece, cover tightly and bake for 18 minutes at 357 degrees uncover and add thyme fresh or dry, broil for 3 minutes and enjoy it.

Sweet Teriyaki Salmon

1 lemon

½ cup teriyaki sauce

3 garlic cloves

3 tablespoons soy sauce

1 hand full of scallion green part only

4 slices of salmon

Directions

- Place the Teriyaki, soy sauce and garlic on a baking sheet.
- Stir around, add the lemon juice and bring the salmon skin on top
- Leave salmon to rest in mixture for 20 minutes or so.
- Flip the salmon and preheat oven to 375 degrees, cover with **** aluminum foil and bake 18 minutes, uncover and broil 3 minutes.
- Cut the scallion into circles and decorate your fish, serve and enjoy.

Fish with Cornflake Crumbs

2 cups cornflake crumbs

3 eggs

6 slices of flounder fish or any fish of your choice

2 tablespoons dry parsley

1 tablespoon garlic powder

1 table spoon paprika

½ teaspoon salt

1 cup of flour

3 cups of cooking oil

Directions

- Dry fish with a paper towel on a plate combine cornflakes crumbs with parsley,
- paprika, garlic powder and salt
- Place them apart.

- On a separate plate take the fish and cover each side with the flour coating very well.
- On another place whisked eggs and bring coated fish to the eggs making sure the fish is very well coated with the eggs, bring the coated fish to the cornflakes mixture and finally place oil on a frying pan, bring them to the flames on medium high, when oil is hot fry fish 3 minutes each the side or till fish is golden brown, place them on paper towel to remove excess oil and enjoy this with your favorite smashed potatoes.

Fry Fish
Daucen Style

6 – 3 small snapper or grouper gutted or
long cuts of fish
½ teaspoon of dry oregano
3 crushed garlic gloves
½ teaspoon of pepper
1 teaspoon coarse sea salt to taste
4 cups of oil for frying
2 limes cut into wedges
3 tablespoons of cornstarch

Directions

- Pat dry with paper towel. Sprinkle each fish with oregano, garlic and pepper, add salt. Briwsh each fish with the cornstarch, followed by salt and pepper making sure it gets into the cuts.
- Bring oil to a frying pan on medium flames, when oil is very hot fry each side till the fish is golden brown, place on paper towel to dry excess oil, serve with tostones or moro de guandules.

Salmon a la Ajonjoli

4 slices of salmon
1 cup of soy sauce
½ cup teriyaki sauce
¼ sesame seeds
½ teaspoon garlic powder
½ teaspoon onion powder
½ teaspoon paprika
½ table spoon lemon juice

Directions

- Brush each piece of salmon with lemon juice and teriyaki sauce, sprinkle with paprika, garlic powder and onion powder, finally cover with the sesame seed. Afterwards place them on parchment paper and baking sheet and cover very tightly.

- Preheat oven to 375 ° degrees. When oven reaches the right temperature bake fish for 15 minutes and uncover in 7 minutes.

- Place a small portion of sauce in a serving bowl adjusting fish on top, serve this on special occasions with your favorite combination.

Scallops with Sweet Sauce

2 pounds of scallops on chunks

1 cup of BBQ sauce

½ teaspoon salt

1 ½ small onion on big circles

½ teaspoon garlic powder

½ teaspoon paprika

1 cup mayonnaise

½ sugar

1 cup of ketchup

½ teaspoon of parsley flakes

½ tablespoon onion powder

Directions

- Place fish over paper towel to dry excess water.

- On a baking sheet place parchment paper, add onion, paprika,
- garlic powder, onion powder and salt cover very tightly and bake onions at 400 degrees for 15 minutes.
- Bring out onions, now place fish on top of onion. Brush it with BBQ sauce very well on each side bake uncover ed now at 375 degrees for 25 minutes.

- In a bowl mix mayonnaise, sugar, ketchup and parsley flake pour this sauce under your fish and now enjoy it.

Salmon with Olives

4 slices of Salmon
1 yellow pepper diced
1 egg tomatoes diced
1 tablespoon of soy sauce
1 tablespoon of honey
½ tablespoon garlic powder
½ tablespoon paprika
½ cup green sliced olive
½ teaspoon salt
½ teaspoon onion powder
juice of one lemon

Directions

- In a baking sheet arrange salmon over parchment paper. Pour all spices on top, add yellow pepper and tomatoes, pour honey and soy sauce, add green olives and lemon juice, preheat oven at 375 degrees. When it reaches the right temperature stick salmon to bake for 20 minutes covered very tightly. Finally, uncover and broil 2 minutes, bring out and serve with rice or salad.

CPSIA information can be obtained
at www.ICGtesting.com
Printed in the USA
BVHW021107190321
602996BV00001B/2